Train inner strength & will-power

How to find a self-determined and happy life without inner blockages with effective mental training - incl. the best tips & exercises

Cornelius Berger

CONTENT

What you can expect in this book

There are people who have a precise plan of how they will consistently achieve their goals and leave no doubt whatsoever that they will actually do it. They don't let anything stop them, neither unforeseen setbacks nor other obstacles. They find a solution to every problem and grow from the challenges they face. Other people, on the other hand, have none of these qualities and therefore quickly feel overwhelmed or unable to rise to a situation in the first place. Now we come to the question, what is the crucial difference between them?

The answer is: mental strength

It is an attribute that not everyone possesses, but can be learned by everyone. In the following chapters you will learn everything you need to know about mental strength and how you can best train it, use it and ultimately achieve completely new successes in all areas of life.

What exactly is mental strength?

Mental strength is a term that contains a whole smorgasbord of positive qualities and it may even mean something to you, but what really and truly lies behind it, most will only be able to guess. First of all, let's address the question: what exactly is mental strength? The definition of it is relatively easy to explain:

Mental strength is a skill that helps you to perform optimally and make success-oriented decisions, regardless of what influences you are currently exposed to. When dealing with difficult or stressful situations, it helps to be mentally strong in order to act in a more relaxed and confident manner. Mental strength is therefore synonymous with emotional stability. The general term comes from the colloquial language, but in the meantime there are also quite a few scientific as well as psychological definitions for it, which you will learn more about later. Very often, predominantly in the origin, one used this term particularly in the sporty context. The actual basic idea was the following: Athletes of any kind who possess mental strength have a great advantage in competition over their opponent. Mental strength is therefore a decisive factor that can determine victory and defeat. At least that was the assumption.

WHAT MAKES IT STAND OUT?

By now, you must be wondering how this mental strength is distinguished in order to really recognize it as such? Researchers have intensively surveyed athletes and agreed that one very decisive characteristic was repeated among the respondents, and that is a firm belief in oneself and one's own abilities. Also, the unshakable will to always achieve one's goals. Giving up is not an option, in keeping with the principle of "fall down, get up, keep going."

You have probably already noticed that one's own self-confidence and stamina always come up and are the cornerstone for recognizing and developing mental strength. The foundation, of course, also consists of a particularly strong desire to succeed. There is a whole package of other qualities that go with it. For example, the useful ability to focus on the task at hand, despite distractions and interruptions, and not to allow any distractions. It is also particularly important not to lose psychological control of yourself in the first place after a negative or surprisingly demanding situation, and if you do, to regain it. Many mentally strong people are also characterized by the fact that they manage to go beyond their own physical as well as emotional limits and still do not lose sight of their goal. Mental strength means being able to allow fears, but without letting them guide or determine one's actions. Overall, it can be said that mentally strong people have an extremely high frustration tolerance, face hurdles with an extra portion of willpower, and can keep their focus on their goals despite stress, hectic and nerve-racking situations.

Perhaps you have discovered a characteristic already mentioned that also applies to you.

WHAT IS MENTAL STRENGTH NEEDED FOR?

Now you have already roughly got what mental strength is for, but what you actually need it for will be explained in detail in the following text. There is a crucial difference between successful people and those who are less so. It is their willingness to take not the easier path, but the rockier one, packed with possible setbacks and obstacles. Mentally strong people face challenges rather than shrink from them, and decide rationally, between right and wrong. They need this strength to spur themselves on. Whether it's healthy eating or relationship problems, mental strength can prove helpful in so many different situations. It helps you keep your cool in any potential crisis, whether professional or personal, and approach your problems with a healthy degree of optimism.

Mentally strong people also find it easier to break through certain blockages. When thoughts play in an endless loop in our mind, overcoming them can often become a real hurdle. In general, thoughts and feelings have a lot to do with mental training. External stimuli trigger reactions and thought patterns in us, which usually start in childhood and are significantly reinforced by our environment. Reaction and thinking patterns are healthy mechanisms, but over the years they store not only useful behavior patterns, but also those that cause us problems in the meantime. It has been proven that our "brain muscle", i.e. a synapse, gains strength with each negative thought pattern and such pathways in our thoughts have a great impact on our emotions and in the long run also on our mental health. They can even affect our immune system and nervous system. Fortunately, this mechanism can be interrupted by building a positive mindset and intensive mental training.

Almost every single area of life is characterized by mental strength, because it has the greatest influence on whether you are successful or not. Thus, mental strength is an essential key factor for your personal happiness, but also to make your own life easier and to master smaller or larger difficulties simply better. Not everyone has the privilege and possesses mental strength from birth. Some find themselves, without giving it much thought, in the above-mentioned characteristics, while others cannot comprehend how their fellow human beings can go through life with such great self-confidence and stamina. The good and essential thing about mental strength, however, is that it can be consciously learned, built up and trained. In the following chapter you will learn more about mental training.

How does mental training work?

You now know what a great role one's own will and also the power of thought play in really achieving one's dreams and goals. Mental strength, no matter how much or little a person possesses of it, is the decisive guidepost in this process and it can be learned, built up and trained by anyone. Mental training includes a whole range of methods aimed at increasing your social as well as emotional competence, resilience, cognitive abilities and self-confidence. It is about increasing your enjoyment of life and the pursuit of contentment and your personal happiness; about turning perhaps long-forgotten dreams or desires into your reality. It also supports you to cope with any kind of stress and helps you to recharge the necessary energy to be able to realize all your plans.

But how does mental training work? Imagine you are learning a dance. This may sound strange at first, but you will soon understand what is behind it. So: You learn the choreography, always one step, one turn more and you repeat the same steps every day, over and over again, until you have analyzed and internalized every movement in detail. This is how mental training works. By regularly and very intensively occupying yourself with the movement sequences in your mind, you become more and more aware of certain details and they become clearer. Your own perception and view of things become sharper.

Just by imagining the movements, your muscles respond with minimal reactions and in general your connections of muscles and nerves are trained. Through the neural networks thus formed, certain courses of action are specifically internalized and even behaviors that you play through in your mind over and over again can contribute enormously to personality development. Our subconscious is activated by the pictorial imagination of a certain state and thus mental training is not only effective in sports alone, but can also be applied in any other possible situation in everyday life.

IN WHICH AREAS IS IT USED?

You can now imagine much more under the term "mental training" and know what effect it can have on your life. But in which areas can it be used consciously? In the already mentioned sports psychology the first applications of mental training took place and even today mental training is used professionally in all sporting areas. In sports, mental training leads to significantly improved concentration and helps enormously in learning movement sequences.

Mental training also has a positive effect at school and can thus solve learning blockades and ensure better handling of difficult situations. It almost sounds like a kind of miracle cure for everything negative, and in a way it is. Nevertheless, it remains a training that must be repeated consistently so that your abilities as well as talents can develop optimally.

WHAT DOES IT CONTRIBUTE TO YOUR PERSONAL DEVELOPMENT?

Most of you are probably familiar with the feeling of being dull and lacking energy at work and not really knowing why you lack the drive that is so important at precisely such moments. Through mental training, you will succeed in your daily tasks much more easily and your motivation will also increase. Another very important aspect is the social environment, where you have to deal with interpersonal problems again and again. Here, too, mental training can be applied.

Self-reflection is one of the most important skills and contributes an elementary part to mental personality development. It is essential for a happy life and the first step in building a healthy self-confidence and defeating self-doubt. This particular skill means observing oneself and being aware of one's thoughts and desires. This mental process is about explaining one's own feelings and thoughts with the help of reasoning.

Structuring one's self-reflection helps to clearly define and fix one's desires. There are some methods that are designed to use external impulses to overcome one's own problems with new thoughts. In itself, it is not possible to approach the methods of self-reflection in the wrong way. The only problem with this could be that you are too critical to yourself and cannot accept motivational phrases. You surely know that everyone has weaknesses and they are part of being human. If you manage to internalize this fact, part of the work is already done. People unfortunately have a bad habit of not staying on the ball. However, continuous work on yourself is crucial for future success. So you see, it takes a certain amount of discipline to really implement self-reflection.

There is a kind of self-knowledge exercise sheet. It helps you reflect on your beliefs, emotions and your tendencies in how you react to certain situations. This can be useful as a guide for your next steps, it is very quick and you don't have to do anything except answer as truthfully as possible.

Ask yourself what your greatest talents and abilities are, then which of your talents and abilities fill you with pride and satisfaction. Next, you need to ask yourself what special traits and characteristics you admire in other people.

And last but not least: What skills do you wish you could develop?

At first glance, some of these tasks may seem redundant, but that varies from person to person. Also, these questions are designed to help you focus on the things that are important for your future life. Once the practice sheet is finished, keep it in a safe place and let what you have written sink in. After a few weeks, you can take the sheet out again and read your answers, and then focus entirely on what your response will be.

The best thing would be to let self-reflection become your routine. You should not just self-reflect once or twice, but repeat the exercises at regular intervals. Create a clear rhythm that trains your mental strength. Self-reflection requires little time and can generally be easily accommodated in everyday life.

Mental training therefore contributes a lot to your personal development. Focusing on certain goals also strengthens your own will to win. Your belief in yourself will be increased, your mind will recover from failures much easier and you will be able to face new challenges much faster. Earlier it was mentioned that mental training can also be applied in any everyday situation.

HOW CAN MENTAL TRAINING BE INTEGRATED INTO EVERYDAY LIFE?

Did you know that about 60,000 to 70,000 thoughts run through our heads every day? A whole sea of impressions, feelings and considerations that rushes through our bodies. This number is large and powerful. But of this large and powerful number, of all our thoughts, a full 86 percent are negative and only 14 percent are positive or constructive.

Your thoughts have the most formative influence on your life, this is a fact that should not be suppressed. Our thoughts determine and direct our actions and our actions determine our behavior. As you can probably guess, our behavior determines our entire life. The crucial thing here is that you must not let yourself be guided by negative beliefs. Sentences such as: "I can't do it", "I'll never make it", or "I'll never be good enough", should from now on be deleted from your vocabulary and above all from your thoughts, because otherwise you will never be able to fully exploit your potential and your goals will be considerably more difficult to achieve. If such negative thoughts do arise, stifle them with a positive one and spur yourself on inside: "You can do it!"

One exercise that should help you do this is to examine your own thoughts. Take enough time to do this.

Ask yourself what is most on your mind right now, what you have to think about a lot, and whether your thoughts are more positive or negative. Then ask yourself how you deal with yourself or how you talk to yourself. Now comes the last question: What feelings come up during your inner conversation with yourself?
Take a pencil and write down the answers in bullet points over the period of about a week. The notes need to be sorted into supportive and restraining thoughts. Be sure to record positive affirmations you say to yourself in particularly

challenging situations. Repeat these words over and over again.

Of course, negative thoughts cannot be avoided in the long run; there is no button you can push that will banish everything bad from our minds. What you can do, however, is to replace your negative attitude with a positive one and keep it that way. This works very well with affirmations. A so-called "affirmation" is a positive phrase that, if repeated very regularly, has the power to change your negative thoughts. For example, if you say to yourself over and over again, "I am self-confident," your mind internalizes that. In this way, you create your own personal earworm that serves as an anchor for your subconscious.

How to train your mental strength

DIFFERENT TYPES OF MENTAL TRAINING

There are many different types and numerous forms of mental training. One of the best known will probably be familiar to you, because this is meditation. Perhaps you have already had some experience with meditation and know that the real goal is to achieve absolute stillness and inner emptiness. Meditating is an extremely effective way to calm down as well as recharge your batteries and get rid of stress and other negative thoughts. Even in medicine, meditation is recommended for insomnia, among other things, and has even been proven to help with high blood pressure. During meditation you train your mind to be more composed and calm and to focus on yourself.

Then there is autogenic training. This method is aimed at relaxation and calm, and also to help improve concentration. You go through certain sentences in your mind that relax and strengthen the body at the same time. Autogenic training generally challenges stress tolerance and in some cases helps with chronic pain. This training is a relaxation method based on autosuggestion. This was developed from hypnosis by Berlin psychiatrist Johannes Heinrich Schultz and was first officially presented in 1926. But for some people this kind of training is not suitable, for example for people suffering from schizophrenia, because this strong concentration could possibly trigger delusions. This exercise can also possibly cause anxiety in hypochondriacs.

The affirmations already mentioned are also an effective exercise, or selected mantras. A mantra is a word or a whole verse. Mantras consist of certain sounds and rhythms that aim to release positive energies. An affirmation, on the other hand, works similarly to a mantra, but instead of working on a sound level, it works more on a thought level. They are phrases that are tailored to you and are usually short, but they can do great things. They can be found in yoga and also in other spiritual teachings. Even if you have not had any real contact with these areas, you can use affirmations or mantras to strengthen your mindset and acquire a positive and open basic attitude.

The thought patterns, beliefs and convictions you have created for yourself play a special role in training yourself to have a more open attitude. It is human nature to always think one's own thoughts as the only true ones first, leaving little room for others or new opinions.

Through certain experiences in childhood or adolescence, negative impressions and beliefs can be formed that help determine the rest of your life. In some situations, there is then a kind of echo of these negative principles, which may then make you doubt your own intelligence. Something like this can also manifest itself in the fact that you think you are not good enough, or place an increased value on what other people think of you, and thus do not behave like yourself.

These thoughts are precisely the problem, because they represent an enormous obstacle that limits you in your desire to grow and also inhibits your daring. In everyday life, these thoughts can have a paralyzing effect and greatly affect your self-esteem. This is exactly where affirmations and mantras come into play. Through them, the brain can be trained by feeding it optimism and positive thoughts, which then replace our negative beliefs through constant repetition. It's not easy to convince your brain to simply rearrange its thoughts, but it is possible. The key here is again repetition. It takes perseverance and patience to do this, but sentence by sentence, the meanings that lie within are internalized and thus an absolutely positive mindset is built.

Another option is the mindfulness exercises. Through this exercise, you train your mind to focus on only one thing. Also, you train your conscious experience. These exercises are supposed to help reduce stress. As a rule, they are easy to perform without any special tools, which is why they can be easily integrated into everyday life. Mindfulness exercises are various techniques designed to help reduce stress and improve self-awareness. The point is to experience the "here and now" more consciously. In this context, mindfulness means the personal willingness to accept what comes one's way, entirely without pejorative or approving feelings. It is about pure acceptance of a thing. In Buddhism, mindfulness exercises have a very high value.

Especially for people whose everyday life includes a lot of stress and hectic, mindfulness-based stress reduction is suitable, but basically everyone can try these exercises, the important thing is that you take the exercises seriously and are generally open to the method.

Besides the already mentioned mediation and mindfulness, visualization is also a popular method. In classical meditation, we mainly pay attention to our own breath and the sensations we feel while doing so. With visualization, on the other hand, you concentrate on the inner images. You consciously imagine the situations you want to experience in reality. The brain does not distinguish between reality and imagination when processing images. This is a fact that can be useful during visualizing to specifically imagine desired outcomes. Visualization is often used before falling asleep, because during this time one is in a very relaxed state. This technique is also used in the field of professional sports. The benefits that regular practice of visualization can have are shown by an experiment conducted by the Australian psychologist Alan Richardson: he divided a basketball team into three groups. The question was how many free throws the individual players could shoot. The first group had twenty minutes per day to do this.

The second group was not allowed to train in actual reality, but was only supposed to visualize the free throws. The rest of the players were neither supposed to train in reality nor to visualize. The result was more than impressive. The ability to shoot free throws improved almost as much in the visualization group as in the group that actually trained, while no improvement could be seen in the last group.

Visualization is multifaceted and just as applicable in daily life. It doesn't matter if it's about imagining your next dream vacation in detail or visualizing another wish. Visualizations also serve to reduce stress and contribute to a balanced life.

A 2011 study proved that guided visualization can minimize and alleviate stress-related conditions. Visualizations have been proven to work best when you not only imagine your personal desires, but also try to feel the associated emotions at the same time. This means, for example, if you imagine your desk or workplace is a place where you feel very comfortable, put yourself in the emotional state of joy while visualizing. Through positive feelings, the realization potential of what you visualize increases extremely.

If you use these methods regularly, you will soon feel a positive effect on your life. You can also combine different exercises to further enhance the effect.

Helpful tips and exercises

A variety of different types of the possible exercises have already been mentioned, in the following we will explain you the implementation of them in more detail. At the beginning, the exercises may sound a bit complicated, but basically they are quite simple. Since mental strength can be learned by anyone, strengthening the mind can also be done quite individually. In doing so, it is extremely important to defeat your own self-doubt in advance. Self-doubt is the main reason why people fail to realize their dreams.

At times, everything can go well in our lives, giving us no real reason to question ourselves. But every now and then we still stumble when our own path suddenly changes. These don't always have to be negative changes, they can also be moments of joy, such as the birth of a child, but such an event can also be another reason for self-doubt. The questions of whether one is good enough in one's role as a parent or whether one is doing everything right tempt people to lose their confidence in themselves bit by bit and therefore ultimately to doubt themselves and their decisions.

People always want to meet their own requirements and have a very precise idea of how they should be. However, new or unforeseen situations also require new reactions and actions, and before you make yourself a list of unfulfillable tasks or expectations, you should first focus on them. Unfavorable external influences can be just as much a reason for self-doubt as, for example, a job that does not promise success or a conflict-ridden partnership in which there are often mutual recriminations and quarrels.

If you think about it very carefully, you will realize that a single glance or a thoughtless comment can be enough to stir up self-doubt. Our subconscious reacts to this because we want to please other people and we would otherwise fear that they might turn away. Fear of being alone plays a crucial role here. If self-doubt increases in frequency and intensity, it is advisable to actively do something about it.

You need to see your self-doubts for what they are: Thoughts. Nothing more and nothing less. Your ideas, requirements and entire expectations of yourself exist only in your head. It is solely up to you whether you allow yourself to be so paralyzed by possible scenarios and contingencies that you downright sink into self-doubt, or actively focus on what is actually real. If you notice that your doubts are becoming too powerful or uncontrollable, try gently shaking your head a few times - this can clear the clutter in your thoughts and creates a clearer view of things. Then take a deep breath and name your thoughts, something like this: "I was just thinking that I acted downright stupidly in this situation." The emphasis on "I was just thinking ..." is very important here.

Just because you think something does not automatically mean it is true. They are merely your personal thoughts. If you repeat this exercise, you may find it much easier to distance yourself from negative thoughts. Always remember, self-doubt is often at the beginning of the road, success at the end. So it is completely up to you to figure out which exercises our mind responds to best. Before we get to the actual mental training, here are some tips to help you become mentally strong. Here, determination is of particular importance.

Being goal-oriented means focusing one's thoughts, actions and feelings on a goal over a longer period of time. Goal-oriented people consciously strive towards a target state, and the most important thing is to know what you actually want. You can set out to achieve what you want, but as long as you are half-hearted about it or don't have properly defined goals, you won't achieve any of it. Goals are not just dreams that you can chase blindly.

The essence of purposefulness is the firm intentions to actually implement your planned intentions. For this, sudden spontaneous thoughts are not enough; instead, you need a concrete aspiration for a certain thing. Wishes and goals should also be a matter of the heart and not just defined with the head.

A Canadian study has come to the conclusion that goals prolong our lives. Sounds strange at first, but somehow it makes sense. Carleton University psychologist Patrick Hill found that people with a strong sense of purpose pay attention to living a healthier life, place a greater value on their fitness and are, on balance, happier than those who lack this trait. Now, here are some tips and suggestions that you can use to start exercising your mental strength the right way.

Whether in your private or professional life, having goals is an indispensable part of your own development. If you don't strive for anything, you won't achieve anything. Without knowing an exact path and having the end goal in mind, you will lack an understanding of the level of progress you may have already made and whether you are even following the right course. Without knowing the right course, you will be drowning in the storm of thoughts and changes, sooner than you think. The good thing is that determination is just as learnable as mental toughness. Seek and find the factors that prevent you from succeeding, and eliminate distractions or sources of interference to achieve the optimal level of purpose.

The first tip may be a perennial phrase to your ears that you've probably heard many times before, yet it's very important to your continued endeavors. It is: learn from mistakes. Everyone makes them, and some may make them too often, and everyone knows that subsequent bad feeling that shoots through your body like poison after you make a mistake. But mistakes are exactly what will help you on your way and they are useful to improve yourself. So if you learn not to see your own mistakes or mishaps as just something negative, the first step in the right direction has already been taken. Like an extra memory card, the brain remembers the mistakes that have been made and thus, in concrete situations, you can make the decision to react correctly and not repeat mishaps that have already happened.

The second tip would be to develop a healthy dose of optimism. This does not mean that you should focus exclusively on the positive, however, sincere optimism is simply necessary to get a bit closer to certain goals and to realize one's dreams. You should not immediately view problems as

final obstacles, but as challenges, and motivate y-
ourself by repeatedly saying to yourself "I can do
this!" Optimism is a natural and human trait, as
researcher Shelley Taylor has proven in several
studies. In the process, she developed a concept
that healthy people generally see everything a
little more positively than is actually the case.

Other studies have also concluded that positive thoughts can affect our physical and mental
well-being. In another study, researcher Shelley
examined the basic mental attitude and disease
progression of HIV-infected men. The resulting
findings were more than conclusive. Namely, she
found that sufferers who approached their disease
with confidence remained significantly healthier
than those who approached it with a negative attitude. Those who assumed from the outset that
they would suffer severe or certain symptoms
were also more likely to get them than those who
expected a better or good course. Here, although
the results refer to a very specific disease, there
are many other results that support their thesis of
healthy optimism.

You have to think of your brain as a computer,
with networks and software, and your whole self,

how you talk to yourself and treat yourself, is the program that runs on it. So if you have a strong belief that you are going to get sick, that will be true. It's the same with believing in yourself. If you keep telling yourself that you will never amount to anything and that you will never achieve your goals, your program will run on that and you will never become the person you aspire to be. Your computer is constantly being tapped by your mind, so it is important that you become aware of negative thoughts.

Our brain has two departments: The first is the cerebrum, which is responsible for processing the thousands and thousands of pieces of information we take in every day and coordinating our thought processes. The second division has other smaller brain areas that are considered very old by the evolutionary history of mankind, since we had them before the cerebrum actually began to grow large. These older parts of the brain hold their own against the more rational cerebrum in critical or difficult situations, as if, for example, we were to grab a hotplate we had just used to check it, knowing that it was actually still hot.

In such moments the smaller brain areas are in command and decide dominantly to execute this movement against better knowledge. So you could consider these areas as a kind of control center, because through them most of our automatic body functions are controlled. As you are reading this sentence, you don't have to consciously think about breathing in and out or giving your heart the command to beat, because these certain areas take over these vital tasks for you.

Your nervous system also plays its part, as the autonomic nervous system is predominantly controlled by the small areas of the brain. Vital functions would be forgotten by you or performed incorrectly if your system did not take care of this for you. You can access other functions at will, such as your body movements, because they are controlled with the voluntary nervous system. This nervous system is in turn controlled by the cerebrum. So the autonomic nervous system does not follow the good old adage: "Think first, then act", but does exactly the opposite. As soon as it receives the first impulse, a reaction to it follows immediately, as our system considers it essential for survival.

The voluntary nervous system draws the short straw when it comes to speed and therefore has rather little say in the matter. To explain this process briefly in more detail, here is an example: You are standing in front of a terrarium, watching an adult tarantula, and although you know that you are protected by the glass that separates you from the spider, you flinch as soon as the spider makes a sudden movement. Your autonomic brain thus wants to tell you to take flight, even though your voluntary nervous system is trying to calm you down. This instinct dates back to the Stone Age, when there were no glass screens to protect us from wild animals.

So, no matter what tasks these two opposing systems are performing, it always ends up in thought processes or body reactions for yourself. Therefore, it is advisable to strengthen yourself mentally also for such reactions of the body. A positive mindset is one of the most important components of mental strength.

The third tip is to learn from others and be happy about your successes. Sometimes people need to look at others to understand certain situations and build an inner strength. Try not to feel envy or be begrudging when you notice other people around you celebrating their successes. Envy only occurs when the feeling of not being good enough takes over and you start comparing yourself to others. At its worst, this emotion can lead you to minimize the successes of those around you, or even tempt you to intentionally boycott their successes. At its best, however, this emotion can serve as a motivator and cause you to work on or even excel at yourself. You might even take these people as role models and be inspired by their breakthroughs. True to the motto: If others have done it, you can do it too.

The fourth tip is to admit your fears and weaknesses. A weakness can be many things, for example a physical inability or a moral and character imperfection. In the course of our lives, based on certain statements from our parents or experiences in childhood, we develop a very personal standard against which we measure ourselves again and again. Added to this are the demands and influences from the media, which are far removed from reality and further increase our own insecurities. In order to be able to accept weaknesses, it is important to know and reflect on yourself well. Ask yourself what it means for you to be weak and also allow these weaknesses, because it is completely human. Observe what difficulties could lead you off your path and stand by your weaknesses as well as your fears. Work on them specifically and you will see and, above all, feel success.

The fifth tip is all about being aware of your own emotions. People quickly fly into a rage in certain situations, react irrationally and, in retrospect, get angry about not having handled a conflict or situation differently. Emotions obscure one's view of things, as you may also have noticed at certain moments, and that is why it is all the more important to consciously realize one's own emotions so that a more just and adjusted behavior is possible. Emotions are a very personal guide for us humans, even if it is often difficult to correctly interpret or perceive the many different feelings.

Emotions cause certain physical changes to appear and certain behaviors to emerge. They coordinate the different biological systems of the body: degree of tension, facial expression, muscles, nerves and hormones to keep the body ready to react. However, if this rhythm of the body is ignored and feelings are constantly suppressed, this readiness becomes confused and proper action is no longer possible. By suppressing the feelings, the body can even become ill in the long run. So, who really lives his feelings and gives them expression, also takes care of himself and his health.

You have to think of mental strength as a kind of muscle and the more you train this muscle, the stronger it becomes. This is also where the name "mental training" can be derived from. However, for mental training it is not enough to just go to the gym and train your muscles there. In order for you to seriously implement mental training, some steps that will help you to do so will now be explained.

First, this task aims to address smaller challenges. These can vary incredibly depending on the person. You can start with a slightly easier first step, such as taking a cold shower every morning. This beginning can quickly become a well-practiced routine. Another item on the list is to learn to say no. No one likes to turn down someone else's wish or thinks it's great to turn down invitations. This is precisely why people say "yes" far too quickly and don't question whether they really want it until it's too late. Adults in particular are constantly hectic and under pressure, which is why they don't take the time they need to question certain patterns of action.

At the same time, you should always decide for yourself how you want to spend your time and not let yourself be influenced by others. A well-intentioned piece of advice to people who find themselves in what has just been said: Take three deep breaths before you come to a decision or answer.

Likewise, getting up early every day or riding your bike to work can be a challenge. If you keep setting yourself smaller challenges, then you will become mentally stronger day by day. However, the challenges should be neither too small nor too big, because if you consider them too small, then it is not really a challenge, and if they are too big, you will not manage to master them again and again in the long run.

The second task could be a feedback mindset that is right for you. In doing so, you must be careful to accept setbacks and keep trying again, because just because something didn't work the first time doesn't mean it never will. When you learned to ride a bike and fell the first time, you most likely got back up and tried again too. The bigger your goals and aspirations are, the bigger the problems that come with them will be, but they are solvable with the right mindset. As I said, a setback is not a reason to give up, just sometimes you need to change your strategy in order to move forward.

The third step is to lower expectations and accept that things are not always easy. It is often the case that people are quickly discouraged by expectations that are too high, because in reality things often turn out to be more difficult than expected. Whether you are aiming for a promotion or personal development, nothing in life is just given to you and you should never expect the path to your goals to be easy. There is a good guideline that some may or may not want to follow. This is: hope for the best, expect the worst and take it as it comes.

The fourth step is to look at your own feelings rationally. Up to a certain point, you can control your feelings, but this is where it gets a bit tricky again, because this is where mental strength plays a very big and decisive role, even though mentally strong people naturally feel sad, invalidated or depressed at times, these feelings do not keep them from their actual goal. In most cases, it is not just the negative feelings that are the problem, but one's own evaluation of them. When the evaluation about oneself becomes too harsh or when we are simply unfair to ourselves, we start to get stuck in one thing. Quickly one sees oneself as a failure and gets the oppressive feeling of not achieving what one actually wanted to achieve. This is why control over one's emotions is of great importance, because without it we quickly drift into a kind of hysteria and it becomes increasingly difficult to build up inner stability.

The fifth step: Don't try to please everyone. Of course, it is a very good quality if you have empathy and thus pay attention to the feelings of your fellow human beings, however, it should not become a habit that you only act according to what the others around you want from you. Above all, you should never give your consent to everything just to avoid conflicts or arguments. Such behavior requires a high price, as your health and also your relationships will suffer massively.

It also exhausts the mind, because constantly trying to please everyone is exhausting and leads us to create a negative self-image of ourselves. Your inner light flickers more and more until it possibly goes out completely.

What do we learn from this? Be willing to disagree with other people when necessary. Don't try to please everyone, and accept that not every person will like you. So this exercise is designed to help you value your own opinion more than the opinions of others. People will treat you how they want, if you let them. Try to have the greatest respect for yourself.

The sixth step is intended to help you develop the right habits. Everyday habits are common to just about everyone on this earth, whether it's always getting up at the same time, putting the dishwasher away in a certain pattern, or singing loud and crooked in the shower: It is just as much a habit of people to try to achieve their targeted goals only by sheer force of will. While this power is strong and often abundant, it is not constant or reliable, and certainly not inexhaustible. Successful people do not rely on their strong will alone; instead, they develop the right habits.

There are good habits and bad habits. The good ones help you become the person you want to be. The bad ones fight against that aspiration and keep you from reaching your full potential and try to get in the way of your personal growth. Start trying to weed out your habits. Don't get too hung up on a single point or goal, and consider what good habits can serve as supports.

The seventh and final step revolves around focusing only on what you can actually control. You train your mental strength when you focus exclusively on the things that are also within your power. Putting your focus on something you can neither influence nor change will weaken your mental strength. People learn through feedback. By focusing on the things that can be controlled, you overcome personal weaknesses, change and achieve your goals, and it is through this that the brain realizes it has some control. It is solely in y-our power how you appear to other people and how you appear to them, however, you have no power over whether they feel sympathy for you. You alone can determine and control how you raise your children, but it is not in your hands what they do with their lives.

In conclusion, put your focus concretely on the things you can influence and do not waste your energy on other, uncontrollable projects or ideas. Your time is too precious and valuable to hold on to something that has no perspective.

Here's an additional suggestion that some people will be very fond of, but will discourage others: Write a diary. Yes, it is old-fashioned, but it works. Even if this method sounds a bit trite or used up at first, some successful and happy people swear by this very tip. Through regular diary entries, you share your feelings, worries and fears and can try to permanently banish them from your mind. In your written words, you can release everyday frustrations, which can help you achieve inner peace and relaxation. Diaries help to track and evaluate personal developments and increase the chances of success, since goals written down are more likely to be achieved than if they existed merely in thoughts. In addition, this way you document your life phases, which gives you the opportunity to describe situations in which you have demonstrated mental strength and thus have them in front of your eyes again. This way you can increase your self-confidence and mental strength.

Typical mistakes in mental training

Mental training is a very routine procedure, the comparison with a choreography has already been described. A certain number of people, which is possibly not so small, decides to become mentally stronger and wants to train them optimally. At the beginning of the whole thing, these people are really bursting with motivation, but unfortunately it flags again relatively quickly in the first few weeks. Many may wonder whether mental training is something for them at all, and even come to the conclusion to leave it alone, because it doesn't seem to work for them. It has nothing to do with the training, but with their approach, which was wrong from the beginning. As with any other workout, it's important to have a plan and structure in place before you start. So the first big mistake is not having clear goals.

A training plan is always based on your starting position and, of course, on your clear goal that you want to achieve. Exactly the same applies to your mental training plan. Before you start, you need to be clear about a few things, such as in which areas you want to get stronger and, as just mentioned, what your goals are. You should be aware of your strengths and weaknesses and know which mental hurdles to overcome.

Mistake number two is to ignore one's weaknesses. Every person would probably like to forget that personal weaknesses exist at all and devote themselves only to their strengths, however, such a thing is not advisable. The various training sessions are usually fun and offer the chance to develop one's strengths even further. In the long run, however, the weaknesses should also find a place in the training plan, because these must eventually be overcome. It is a process until this also succeeds properly. But as soon as this process is complete, personal development progresses much faster.

The third mistake probably applies to a higher percentage of people. This is not having patience. With physical training, success or progress is more foreseeable, while with mental training it can take much longer before you feel tangible success. Our brain needs a certain period of adaptation, the head needs to be trained and this takes a lot of time and energy. In the first step, you should allow yourself about three months and then evaluate whether noticeable progress has been made.

The fourth mistake is to evaluate developments from day to day. You may be familiar with the saying, "Try to be one percent better every day than you were yesterday." Basically, the intention of this advice is not so wrong, as it should spur you to improve every day. However, the one percent thing is not well thought out, since you can rarely measure improvement in percentages, and especially not in a single one. Moreover, if you follow this advice, your frustration could increase significantly, further stretching what little patience some people have, because it's hard to see success based on a daily comparison. However, if you compare every four or six weeks, you will notice significant differences and improvements.

The fifth mistake that is often made is to train mentally only within your own four walls. Of course, your own home is the perfect comfort zone, you are undisturbed and can fully concentrate on yourself without being irritated by annoying or distracting noises. But it is an essential part of mental training to leave your comfort zone and expose yourself to outside influences, otherwise you would never succeed in overcoming any obstacles and grow from them. There will hardly be any challenge waiting for you in your living room, at least none that will really challenge you. The various influences of life are loud, brutal and full of distractions, but essential for your further journey to build and train your mental strength.

Trying to defeat your own head with, well, your own head is another mistake. Many problems can be solved on a mental level, but this involves an extraordinary amount of effort. In the moments when you almost lose yourself in your own thoughts, you should try to relax your mind and take your body to help you. Our mind can be the purest maze, but the body can show us the way out again.

If your mind ever gets busy with a flood of thoughts, try taking a deep breath and keeping the focus entirely on your breathing. Take steady, definite breaths. Then try to exhale for as long as you can, and you'll feel the chaos in your mind calm down and the fog lift. So both areas have a great influence on each other. You should therefore also know how to use all two.

If you're thinking that this all sounds good and you want to keep it in mind in case you're struggling, you should know that mental training is not for certain occasions. Using mental training only once in a while will bring the same result as doing a work-out for your dream figure only every few months: namely none at all. So mental training isn't there as a rope to pull you out of the hole you've already fallen into, but to keep you from falling into it in the first place. So start now, preferably today, and set clear goals that you consciously want to achieve. Don't push your weaknesses aside and face your fears so you can grow from them. Accept the here and now as it comes.

The differences of mental training in clinical and sports psychology.

You have already learned that the actual origin of mental training is in the sports field and that it is still actively used by athletes. Later, other psychological methods were added to this classical training method, such as attention regulation, self-talk regulation, as well as prediction training and many other methods, which were called mental training. In psychology, the measure of the intensity of attention is concentration. It is about determining the associated inattention to other objects through attention and a certain selection of objects.

Self-talk regulation is another form of mental training. It offers the athlete the possibility to optimize the observation of the body through inner self-motivation and thus to control certain movements. It also promotes self-confidence. Prognostic training is used in sports to learn the right way to deal with mental stress. For this purpose, goals are set in advance and afterwards, after the execution of the task, it is compared whether and how far one has come closer to one's goal.

If the athlete falls short of his or her own expectations, the reasons for this must be determined. The method should enable the athlete to make a realistic self-assessment and to prepare better for possible setbacks. In sports psychology, mental training is applied in such a way that the repetitive imagining of a sports-related course of action is practiced without, of course, performing the action oneself. In this form of mental training, relaxation exercises were combined with visual and auditory imaginings so that the sport psychological requirements could be optimally adapted.

The effect achieved through the improvement of the movement sequence in the conscious imagination should bring about a subsequent improvement in the movements actually executed. Depending on how well the athlete manages to put himself into this illusion, the better the results will be. Here, not only the head but also the body should play an equally important role, because both areas must be in harmony and trained regularly in order to be able to really match the actions with each other. There is a suitable mental and physical level for every action, it is believed. Therefore, this training also focuses on reducing activation through relaxation. Autogenic training and progressive relaxation as relaxation exercises also help here.

Sports psychology assesses the benefits of ambition through the pursuit of success. Depending on the strength of ambition, it can have an active influence on our behavior. People who are performance-oriented have more stamina and don't let setbacks get them down so easily. On the other hand, ambition can also be an obstacle in that our expectations of ourselves no longer correspond to reality. Ambition alone is usually not enough to achieve optimal success. An unconditional acceptance of weaknesses or inhibiting feelings is a prerequisite necessary for retrieving certain achievements, rather than suppressing them through mental training. Each person has only a limited amount of attention and when these resources are used to control the inhibiting feelings, only a limited amount of attention is left for the completion of the actual performance. Therefore, it is an absolute recommendation to accept these feelings as necessary realities in a competitive situation and not to fight against these sensations. Although in this case the athlete puts himself in a demanding situation, this unconditional acceptance leads him to calm down. It sounds paradoxical, but it is a fact. The athlete's acceptance overcomes his fears, sparks new motivation, and develops the courage to face further challenges.

The 4C model is a model that originated in a sports context, but can be applied just as well to other situations. It comes from Clough and Earle and is part of the scientific measurement tool, for mental strength. The four pillars of the model are formed by self-confidence: the firm conviction of one's own abilities. Then challenge: not being afraid of challenges and seeing the opportunity to grow from any hurdles. Control: being convinced of one's own control and seeing events as a consequence of one's actions. The last pillar would be self-commitment: making the achievement of the goal a priority. There were two more factors added to these already known attributes: emotion control and interpersonal trust. Control over one's emotions, also called emotion regulation, is enormously important in controlling them and determining our behavior. Interpersonal trust is defined by representing a certain expectation with certain individuals and being able to rely on promises, whether verbal or written. In everyday life, these factors can act as a support.

Personal attitude is the key to success. Athletes are almost superhumans in certain situations, having to endure a lot of pressure to perform from themselves and their peers. In addition, they have to be fit enough to perform at their best. Their goal is to climb the gold medals and winners' podiums, they want to surpass themselves and enjoy the fact that success seems to magically attract them. Our thoughts are responsible for how we see the world. Athletes use certain thought patterns to visualize and thus conjure up their victory. In business, this method is rarely if ever used, although a certain track record of success could be foreseen. In clinical psychology, however, some of these methods are used and patients therefore have the chance to access quasi untapped resources.

In the new era, mental training is now also used in clinical psychology in the field of psychosomatics. In medicine, psychosomatics refers to a holistic approach and theory of illness. In it, people's reaction patterns and mental abilities in relation to illness and health are considered in their connection with physical processes. In the case of physical illnesses, where psychological factors also have an influence on the healing process, psychotherapeutic procedures are used in certain clinics for healing. People suffering from physical illnesses, such as high blood pressure or chronic pain, often find it difficult to develop the necessary insight to seek psychotherapeutic treatment. However, if the same procedures are offered under the name "mental training," this can increase the willingness of patients.

So the differences in sports psychology and clinical psychology are quite serious after all. In one field, it is exclusively about meeting the expectations placed on oneself through various methods, while in the other, it is about bringing life-enriching treatments to people who might shy away from them without the addition of mental training.

MENTAL TRAINING OR MIRACLES?

You've probably heard about it, or at least read about it, because people still talk about this event today. Flight captain Chesley Sullenberger, 57 years old, made an emergency landing of his Airbus safely on the Hudson River in New York with two failed engines and almost two hundred people on board. He accomplished the impossible, saving exactly 155 lives. The whole world spoke of an undeniable miracle, but from a psychological point of view something quite different had happened: The captain performed this maneuver, showing

how, despite the almost unimaginable circumstances, he accomplished the feat he had been
practicing all these years. Just imagining an action
or movement activates the same brain areas as the
movement itself. So is this a miracle, or is it actually skilled training and proof of real mental
strength?

A happier life with learning mental strength

You have learned all areas of mental training and know what mental strength is needed for and how to train it. It includes an insane amount of repetition, however, also very important and versatile psychological aspects, but also medical and human influences are an essential part of what effect mental strength has and what exactly constitutes it.

You may still be asking yourself why there are such different groups of people. There are those who, despite constant efforts, just can't seem to get anything right and are almost magically attracted to failure. Then there are the people who put their all into it and achieve their goals with a great deal of effort and time invested. Despite their success, these people are then far too exhausted at the end to be able to be happy about having actually made it. Of course, there are also people who achieve all their goals in life with ease and joy, without having made any great effort.

The reason for this is not because of the circumstances from which these people come, nor because of their schooling or what language they may speak. It depends on the mental and emotional level and their personal attitude towards it. Those who understand the mental recipes for success and internalize them can call them up at any time and use them at decisive moments.

A very important emotional law is that all personal power comes from deep within. If we stand in our own way because of negative feelings or distressing thoughts, we will never get to where we want to be, nor will we ever achieve the quality of life we desire. Our emotional world must be in absolute balance and therefore it must stop that we humans make ourselves so dependent on external influences.

When you open your eyes, all around you is a steady stream of people striving for satisfaction and desperately seeking the guidelines for guaranteed success in life, yet they are usually looking in the wrong places, because everything they need to achieve it is already within them. Pretty much everything you need to achieve your goals is within you. It is your own responsibility what thought patterns you allow and whether you can muster the necessary concentration to replace your own negative beliefs with positive ones.
Every person must try to find his own values and live them. You must first recognize your fears and preferences before you begin to actively shape your life. Gaining mental strength can be life-changing for you, perhaps even to the point of quitting your job, moving abroad, or entering into a new relationship. But before any of that can happen, you need to stand up for yourself and focus completely on what you really want. Only then will

you be able to feel and use mental strength without restriction.

www.ingramcontent.com/pod-product-compliance
Lightning Source LLC
Chambersburg PA
CBHW021754150726
47989CB00004B/1663